MONSTER OF THE DEEP

The Louisiana State Museum's Civil War-Era Submarine

by

GREG LAMBOUSY

Director of Collections
Louisiana State Museum

CENTER FOR LOUISIANA STUDIES
University of Louisiana at Lafayette
2006

An earlier version of the text used in this booklet
was published in the Summer 2005 issue of
Louisiana Cultural Vistas magazine;
the Center for Louisiana Studies thanks the
Louisiana Endowment for the Humanities
for permission to reprint it here.

ISBN: 1-887366-70-9

Center for Louisiana Studies
University of Louisiana at Lafayette
P.O. Box 40831
Lafayette, LA 70504-0831

http://cls.louisiana.edu

For more information on the Louisiana State Museum, visit:
http://lsm.crt.state.la.us/

LOUISIANA STATE MUSEUM'S CIVIL WAR-ERA SUBMARINE

The history of the Civil War-era submarine in the collection of the Louisiana State Museum can be traced to 1878, when it was removed from Lake Pontchartrain and placed on the levee by a dredge crew working near the mouth of Bayou St. John. For years after its recovery from the water, the boat lay neglected on the lakeshore. By 1895, it was placed on display at Spanish Fort, a local amusement park, where it became a prominent landmark. A period of neglect followed, during which the submarine was taken from its wooden stand and left lying in the weeds, a remaining propeller blade was removed by vandals, and large areas of loss appeared along the lower hull. Later, in 1908, it was moved to the Camp Nicholls Confederate Home on Bayou St. John. In 1942, the Louisiana State Museum acquired the vessel and moved it to Jackson Square. Some years later, the Museum transferred it into the lower Pontabla Building, where it was featured in a "Defense Exhibit." In 1957, it was moved under the Presbytère arcade.

The question of the vessel's identity has vexed researchers for decades. Many thought the submarine was the *Pioneer*, a vessel constructed in New Orleans by the same group that later built the *C.S.S. Hunley*—the famed submarine now undergoing conservation at the Warren Lasch Conservation Center in Charleston, South Carolina. A sketch of the *Pioneer* discovered in the National Archives by naval historian Mark Ragan demonstrates that the State Museum's submarine and the Pioneer are not the same vessel. The history of the *Pioneer*, however, may nevertheless shed some light on the identity of the State Museum's submarine.

THE C.S.S. *PIONEER*

At the beginning of the Civil War, President Abraham Lincoln ordered a blockade of all Southern ports. To augment his own Navy, Confederate President Jefferson Davis issued a proclamation inviting applications for letters of marque to encourage reprisal against Federal ships and property. Respondents were drawn to the Algiers dockyards (across the river from New Orleans) and to vessels suitable for refitting as privateers. Although much of the activity occurred in secret, some projects were mentioned in the press. References to the *Manassas*, the first ironclad ram, which was outfitted at the John Hughes dry dock in Algiers, appeared in print. At least ten privateering efforts were completed before the occupation of the city.

Algiers Dry Docks, c. 1870,
Photograph by Samuel Blessing.
(Louisiana State Museum)

Across the river at Leeds foundry, located on Foucher and Delord Streets, steam gauge manufacturers James McClintock and Baxter Watson constructed a submarine to use against Union gunboats patrolling Lake Pontchartrain. They would eventually partner with Horace L. Hunley, a wealthy lawyer and customs agent. Hunley, along with prominent New Orleans lawyer Henry J. Leovy and sugar and cotton planter Robert Ruffin Barrow—brother-in-law of Horace Hunley—provided funding for the project. The team built a submarine with a menacing, streamlined appearance. After the war, McClintock described the vessel he and his partners christened the *Pioneer*:

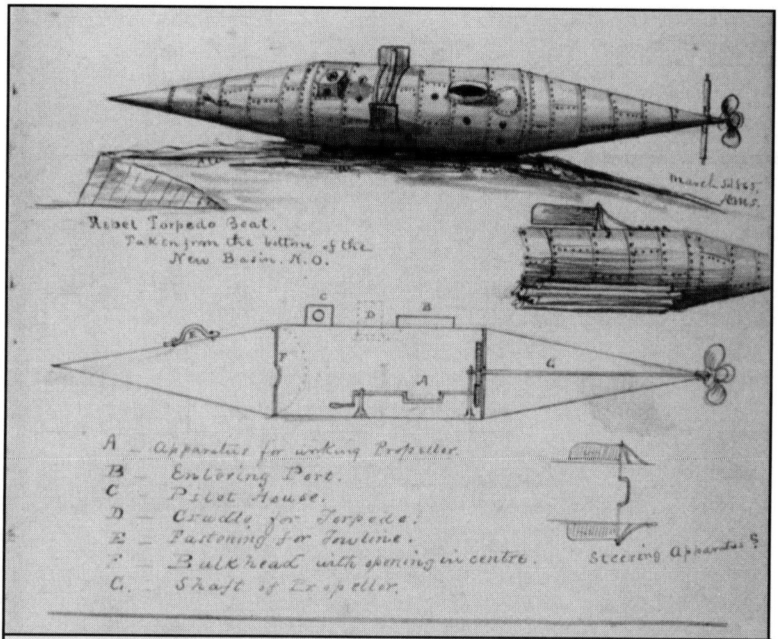

The submarine *Pioneer* sketched by David M. Stauffer as it lay on the bank of the New Basin Canal near Claiborne Avenue, c. 1865. Courtesy the Gilder Lehrman Collection of the New York Historical Society.

> ...she was made of iron 1/4 inch thick. The boat was of a cigar shape 30 feet long and 4 feet in diameter. This boat demonstrated to us that we could construct a boat that would move at will in any direction desired, and at any distance from the surface. As we were unable to see objects passing under the water, the boat was steered by compass...

In March of 1862, the *Pioneer*'s owners were granted a letter of marque by the Confederate government. A month later, New Orleans fell to the West Gulf Blockading Squadron commanded by David Glasgow Farragut. In the ensuing turmoil, the *Pioneer* was scuttled in the New Basin Canal. McClintock, Watson, and Hunley fled to Mobile, where they began work on another project, one that would result in the first submarine ever to sink a ship in battle.

The *Pioneer* was quickly discovered in its watery grave and brought to shore. A Federal team of experts was dispatched to examine the "infernal machine." Team members G.W. Colin and Alfred Baird submitted their

Men associated with the *Pioneer*: (left to right) Charles Leeds, James McClintock, and Robert Ruffin Barrow. (Louisiana State Museum)

measured drawings to Fleet Engineer William Shock, who completed and forwarded them to Washington for further study. Years later, Commander Baird, in a report to the U.S. Naval Institute, recalled his observations:

> [The *Pioneer*] had a little conning tower with a manhole in the top, and small circular glass windows in its sides. She was propelled by a screw, which was operated by one man. She had vanes, the function of which were those of the pectoral fin of a fish. The torpedo was of a clockwork type, and was intended to be screwed from the bottom of the enemy's ship. It was carried on top of the boat, and the screws employed were gimlet- pointed and tempered steel.

The *Pioneer* sat on the bank of the New Basin Canal (which was eventually filled in for construction of the Pontchartrain Expressway) at what would be its present-day intersection with Claiborne Avenue, near the current site of the Superdome, until 1868 when it was auctioned as scrap by the Federal government for forty-three dollars.

A letter from Fleet Engineer Shock to Gustavas Fox, assistant secretary of the U.S. Navy, describes Shock's experience with the *Pioneer* but also includes anecdotal evidence that may actually relate to the Louisiana State Museum's craft.

> Some few weeks since I had some duty calling me to a place down at the 'New Basin' where I discovered a Submarine Machine. I embraced the first favorable opportunity and examined it, got its history and had a drawing made of it, a tracing of which I send you as a curiosity.
>
> The history of the machine seems is simply this. In the early part of Admiral Farragut's operations here the gunboat New London was a perfect terror to the Rebels in the lake, so it occurred to them if

> they could get a Machine that would move underwater, they could succeed in securing a Torpedo to the bottom of the ship, move off, touch the wires, and thus terminate their existence. They finally got the thing done, made a good job of it, got it over board and put two men in it; they were smothered to death.

Since contemporary accounts of the *Pioneer* never mention such a significant incident, it is possible the fatalities reported to Shock occurred in a different experimental craft.

Another contemporary account discovered in the National Archives by Mark Ragan may relate to the Museum's submarine. In June 1861, months before work began on the *Pioneer,* a New Yorker named E.P. Doer on a business trip to Chicago learned from a New Orleans schoolteacher that a submersible to be used against the Mississippi Squadron blockading the river was being constructed. He reported his findings to the Navy in Washington:

> She tells me that the rebels in New Orleans are constructing an infernal vessel to destroy the *Brooklyn,* or any vessel blockading the mouth of the Mississippi; from her description, she is to be used as a projectile with a sharp iron or steel pointed prow to perforate the bottom of the vessel and then explode. Says that it is being constructed by competent engineers. I put implicit reliance in the correctness of this information.

If this letter refers to the Museum's submarine, it would make it the earliest known Civil War-era submersible. However, a hand-powered submarine would have a difficult time navigating the waters of the Mississippi. More likely the craft described by E.P. Doer was designed to operate on the waters of Lake Pontchartrain where the U.S. Navy also had a considerable presence.

SUBMARINE MORTAR

The letter may in fact refer to a 'Submarine Mortar' boat designed by John Roy, an architect who engineered the construction of cannon for the Confederates in New Orleans. The submarine mortar was based on an 1839 design by James Nasmyth, the famous Scottish engineer who invented the steam hammer. Roy's vessel was designed to ram a ship and then discharge an explosive into the hull from beneath the water line. By April 1861, Roy's idea was under consideration by the Confederate government in Montgomery. The boat was described as being much like the *Manassas* except that it was specifically designed as a ram, it could completely submerge, and a gun could be fired from underwater.

In an article published in the *Daily Delta* in late April 1862 the author discusses how the idea for a submarine mortar may have lead to the construction of the *Manassas*.

> The Monster of the Deep—As early as April and May last [1861], Capt. John Roy, of the Smith Artillery, of this city, brought to the notice of the naval authorities the plans for an iron-clad monster, capable of destroying any engine of warfare afloat. It is an English invention to which the Captain added the means of raising and depressing the vessel at will, and a separate apparatus for turning the vessel. The drawings were submitted to Commodore Rousseau and Capt. Semmes of the Sumter, who warmly recommended them to the Navy Department."
>
> The turtle [*Manassas*]," says the [Algiers] *Newsboy*, "was the result of this as a compromise between a perfectly impregnable submarine mortar and a butting boat, the original idea of Mr. Stephenson [Stevenson]. It was built under private auspices by Messrs. Stephenson and Hughes, and a gun to be used above water added. To those improvements Capt. Roy proposes now to add a gun to load under water. The plans are now before the Committee of Safety.

Although the article quoted above later notes that Roy's submarine was never constructed, the Museum's craft could be a working model of the submarine designed by Roy. In fact, Roy experimented with shooting cannons underwater in Lake Pontchartrain.

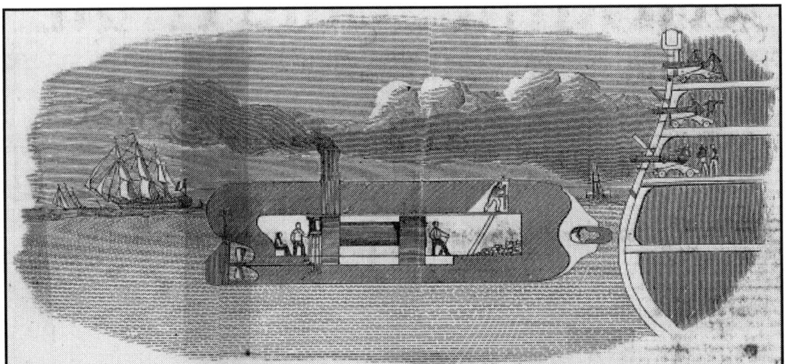

Illustration of the submarine mortar based on an 1839 design by James Nasmyth, the famous Scottish engineer who invented the steam hammer. (*Scientific American*, Feb. 19, 1853)

Louis Gennela, an engineer who studied the Louisiana State Museum craft for many years, theorized that John Hughes, the Algiers shipbuilder, may have built the Louisiana State Museum craft. The submarine was discovered in Lake Pontchartrain near the mouth of Bayou St. John. Hughes owned a shipyard on Bayou St. John and had worked with Roy on a number of occasions during the war. There is also a striking similarity between the structure of the Museum's submarine and the *Manassas* which was definitely constructed by Hughes. Adding credence to the story is a Hughes family legend that John Hughes did in fact build the LSM submarine, although no definitive documentation has yet come to light.

Lending credence to the possibility that the LSM submarine was designed as a kind of submersible mortar is the design of the craft's prow. A tube approximately two feet long and two inches in diameter extends inward from the reinforced cone-shaped prow. However, it seems that the maximum explosive charge that could be generated would be negligible when fired against the hull of a ship, doing little damage. The craft could be a prototype for a much larger submersible that was never constructed, something more on the order of what James Naysmith had originally envisioned.

John Hughes, c. 1880,
Courtesy Mr. David Wilkerson.

By contrast, most believe the Museum's submarine would likely have used a long wooden spar projecting from its prow to carry an explosive charge at its end. The spar would have fit into the tube or socket at the prow of the craft. The vessel would submerge a sufficient distance from the targeted ship, ram the explosive attached to a barbed hook into the ship's hull, then back away a good distance, pulling a wire that set off a fuse in the explosive.

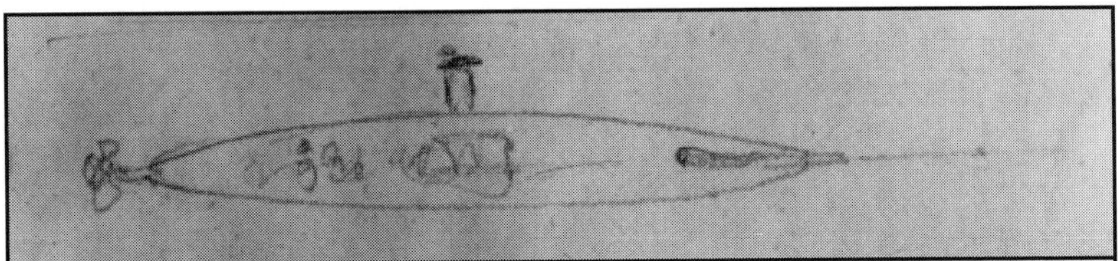

Alfred Waud pencil drawing of an unidentified submarine. Notice the long pole or spar extending from the prow of the vessel. An explosive charge would have been attached near the end of the spar. Courtesy Library of Congress, LC-USZ62-131097.

The Museum's craft is twenty feet long, approximately three feet wide and six feet deep. The iron plates are approximately 1/4 thick, and are fastened to one another with countersunk rivets to increase hydrodynamics. The propeller was likely operated by two men each sitting on brackets attached to opposite sides of the inner hull just under the hatch. They probably would have hand-cranked a differential gear system attached to the propeller shaft. There were two rudders that were operated by the captain or engineer. Both were in the shape of a crescent and were attached to one another by crossed rods. When one was turned the other turned in the opposite direction. Although the rods are now missing, there is just such a design in the U.S. patent records for March 26, 1861, by Ross Winans. The shape of the craft's hull in the patent record is very similar to that of the LSM submarine. There were also two diving planes. A portion of one of them is still attached to the vessel's starboard side. These planes would have been used in conjunction with the intake of water as ballast to submerge and raise the vessel. A brass socket located near the starboard diving plane would allow water to enter the boat. The water could be expelled by means of a pump in order to rise. A stack just forward of the hatch probably had a rubber hose extending from it to the surface of the water to allow for intake of air. The end of the hose would have been held above the surface by a floating piece of wood. It is unclear whether there was a simple, low profile hatch or a conning tower with portholes to allow for light to enter and for sighting. However, candlelight would have been the primary means of illumination and navigation was probably attempted by compass.

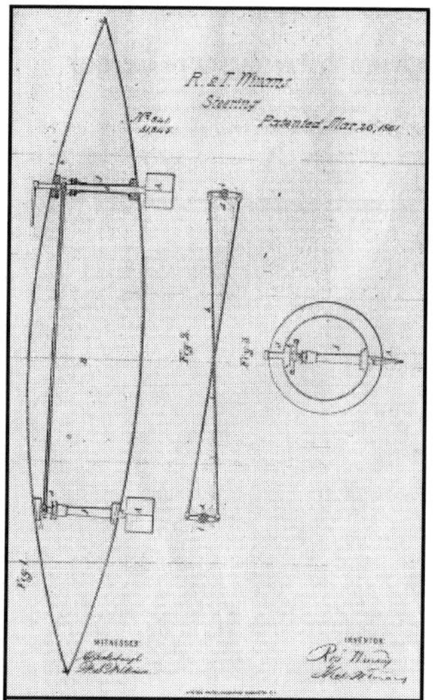

Drawing from the U.S. Patent issued to Ross Winans, March 26, 1861.

THE MYSTERY

The identity of the State Museum vessel remains a mystery. A number of theories have been put forth to account for its origins. Rich Wills, a graduate of the Nautical Archeology Program at Texas A&M University, wrote his thesis on the Museum's submarine. Wills conducted extensive research on Civil War-era submersible vessels and notes that submarines were constructed in various other cities in the Confederacy and that the Museum's submarine could have been sent by rail to New Orleans before the fall of the city or it could have been captured elsewhere, brought to the city and tested in the lake.

Frank Furman, a researcher who has also done a considerable amount of work on the subject, believes that the Museum's submarine may be the submarine shown attacking the S.S. *Minnesota* in an November 1861 *Harper's Weekly* illustration. The profile of the vessel is very similar to that of the Museum's submarine. The *Harper's Weekly* vessel was likely constructed at Tredegar Iron Works, in Richmond, Virginia, and Furman thinks this vessel may have been sent to New Orleans by rail just before the fall of the city. Whatever the case, the Museum's submarine is a very early example of submersible technology.

Considering the present lack of documentation relating directly to the Museum's submarine, it is difficult to make a positive statement regarding the designer's identity. There is, however, no reason to think that the craft could not have been built in New Orleans. The city supported a large foundry business relative to other cities in the South. Work on steamships, sugar refineries, cotton presses, and architectural elements guaranteed that the skills and facilities to build such vessels were available in the city. At least one other submarine was built in New Orleans and there were similar ideas

Caption: A, Propeller.—B, Rudder.—C, Force-pump for ballast.—D, Dead light.—E, Torpedo.—F, Man-hole plate.—G, Cock to let water into the ballast room.—H, Ballast-room.—I, India-rubber suction-plate.—J, India-rubber air-tube.—K, Foul-air pump. SUBMARINE INFERNAL MACHINE INTENDED TO DESTROY THE "MINNESOTA." Illustration from *Harper's Weekly,* November 1861.

being proposed. Most large foundries were in fact employed by the Confederates to manufacture weapons.

Indeed, two Confederate veterans claimed to have knowledge of the construction of the vessel in New Orleans. Francis J. Wehner, a lieutenant in the 5th Louisiana Infantry and a former foundry worker, claimed in a 1924 newspaper interview to have helped build the vessel in New Orleans during the early part of the war, but, unfortunately, the article does not mention any details regarding the designers of the craft or where in the city it was built. Another person who claimed to have knowledge of the submarine was Captain William Youngblood, chief engineer on the ill-fated C.S.S. *Louisiana* and later a boarder at the Camp Nicholls Confederate Veterans Home. In a 1908 *Daily Picayune* interview Youngblood claimed that the vessel was constructed at the Government Yard near the New Basin Canal turnaround by McClintock and Watson. Since McClintock never mentioned constructing a second vessel in New Orleans, Youngblood may have, like others at the time, confused the vessel with the *Pioneer.* Youngblood goes on to note that during an operation in Lake Pontchartrain the vessel submerged but for some reason failed to rise and the crew perished. The vessel, according to Youngblood, was never named.

In another case, Larry Pearson, a descendent of James Drummond, a Scotsman who owned a partnership in the New Orleans foundry Drummond, Doig, & Co., tells of a family legend that James Drummond constructed the Museum's submarine in his facility at 125 Front Street. As of yet, no evidence exists to corroborate the story, but Drummond's foundry would have been capable of producing such a craft.

Hopefully in the future evidence will come to light that will allow us to positively identify the immediate circumstance under which the craft was conceived and fabricated.

The Louisiana State Museum has provided metal samples from the vessel for testing to Alicia Caporaso, a doctoral student with the School of Oceanography, University of Rhode Island. Caporaso is also currently working with oceanographer Robert Ballard to discover a means of preserving the metal structure of the *Titanic*. In the past Caporaso has conducted metallographic studies of ordinance excavated from Civil War-era sites for the National Park Service, comparing the differences between the samples to determine a number of factors including techniques of manufacture. Caporaso will be examining the microscopic structure of the Museum's submarine metal samples to determine their composition. Metal from period foundries from around the country will be tested and compared to the Museum's submarine samples.

In 1999 the submarine was moved from the Presbytère arcade to International Artifacts, Inc. conservation laboratory where conservation of the vessel was conducted by the team of Lynn Harrington, David Johnson, and Herb Bump.

Large portions of the vessel's lower hull had completely deteriorated from a combination of corrosive agents. At some point, probably in the 1930s, previous custodians of the submarine poured concrete into the hull in a misguided attempt to retain the vessel's overall structure. However, it caused the hull to corrode. Extracting the concrete was one of the more difficult aspects of the conservation project, but as the concrete was poured over successive, separating layers of sheet metal and wire mesh, the layering effect somewhat facilitated its removal. All of the concrete has been removed from the lower hull. Mechanisms used to control the aft and forward rudders that were formerly hidden have been exposed. Also uncovered were three gear-like objects, each approximately one foot long, embedded in portions of the keel. The remains of a wooden beam running the length of the keel were also found following removal of the concrete. Samples of the wood were sent to the U.S. Forest Products Laboratory for analysis. Unfortunately, the condition of the wood prevented researchers from identifying the species.

The corrosive effects of the concrete are dramatically visible. Large areas of the rudder shafts expanded from the high moister content of the cement, encrusting them with rust at almost twice their original size. Portions of the keel and hull exhibited similar effects, with the lower hull missing most of its original plating. Stabilization of these areas has now been addressed including reinforcement of fragile areas and a protective coating applied to all of the artifact's parts.

SUGGESTED READING LIST

Campbell, R. Thomas. *The C.S.S H.L. Hunley: Confederate Submarine*. Shippensburg, PA: Burd Street Press, 2000.

Lambousy, Greg. "A Mystery of the Deep." *Louisiana Life* 21 (Summer 2001): 72-74.

Perry, Milton F. *Infernal Machines: The Story of Confederate Submarine and Mine Warfare*. Baton Rouge: Louisiana State University Press, 1985.

Ragan, Mark K. *The Hunley: Submarines, Sacrifice, & Success in the Civil War,* rev. ed. Charleston, SC: Narwhal Press Inc. 1999.

———. *Union and Confederate Submarine Warfare in the Civil War*. Mason City, IA: Savas Publishing. 1999.

———. *Submarine Warfare in the Civil War*. Cambridge, MA: Da Capo Press, 2002.

Wills, Richard K. "The Confederate Privateer *Pioneer* and the Development of Confederate Submersible Watercraft." *The Institute of Nautical Archaeology Quarterly* 21 (Spring/Summer 1994): 12-19.

———. "The Louisiana State Museum Vessel: A Historical and Archaeological Analysis of an American Civil War-Era Submersible Boat." M.A. Thesis, Texas A&M University, August 2000.

The Azby Fund and the Institute for Museum and Library Services generously awarded grants totaling $84,400 to the Louisiana State Museum for the submarine conservation project.

Anyone with photographs or other documentation pertaining to the history of the Louisiana State Museum submarine is asked to contact the museum:

Louisiana State Museum
Director of Collections
1000 Chartres Street
New Orleans, LA 70116

(504) 599-1946
http://lsm.crt.state.la.us/

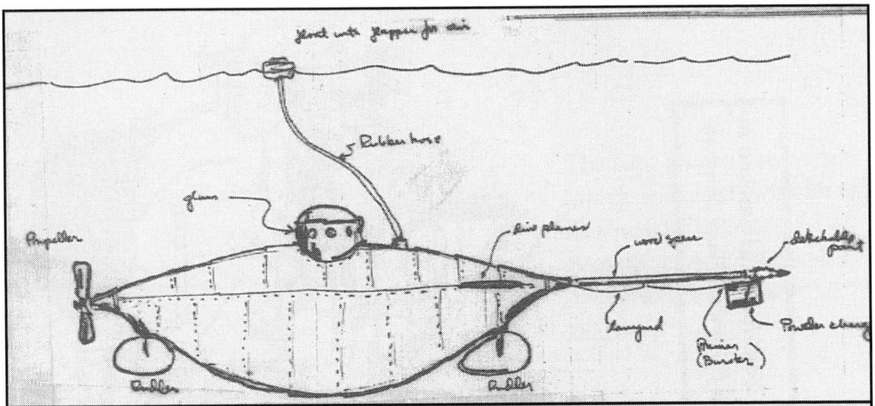

A drawing of the Louisiana State Museum submarine by historian Sidney H. Schell.

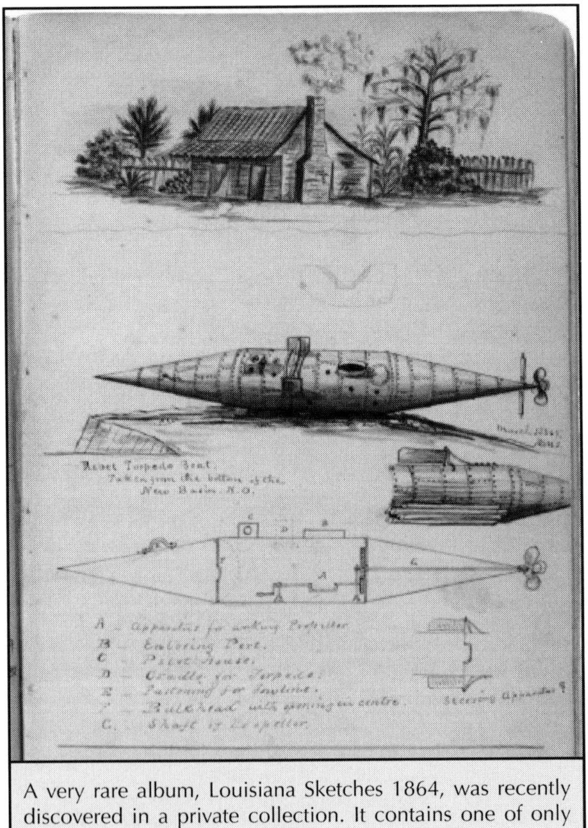

A very rare album, Louisiana Sketches 1864, was recently discovered in a private collection. It contains one of only two known drawings of the *Pioneer*.

Courtesy the Gilder Lehrman Collection of the New York Historical Society.

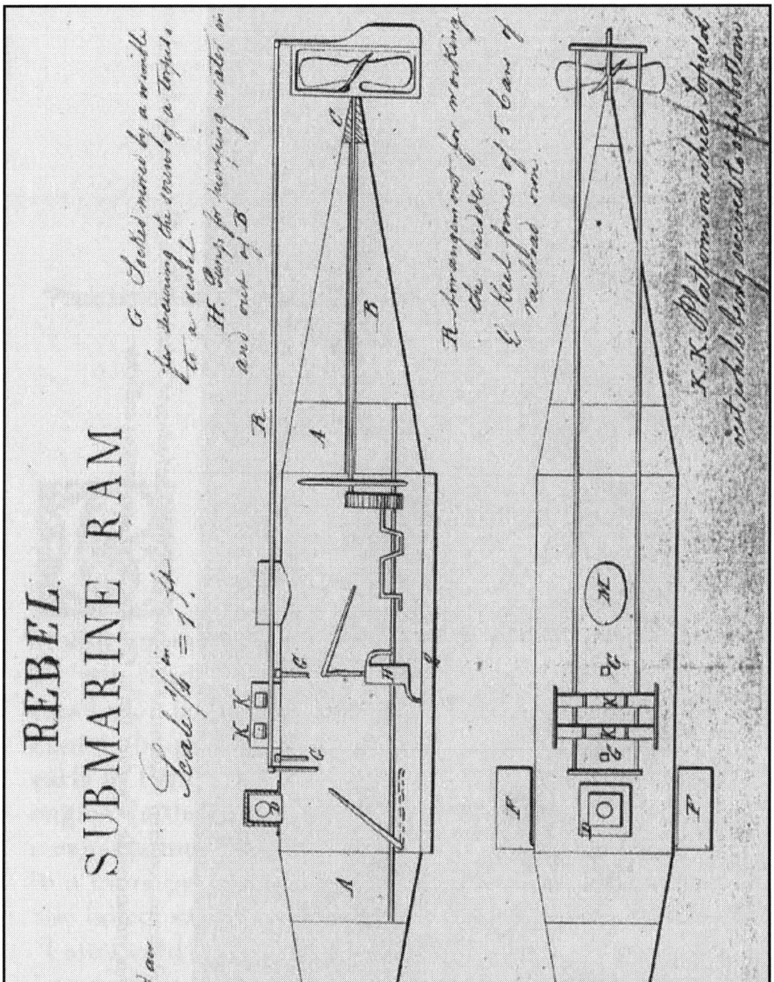

C.S.S. *Pioneer* drafted by engineer William Shock of the U.S.S. *Pensacola*, 1862. (National Archives)

The ironclad ram *Manassas* under fire at Forts Jackson and St. Philip, April 24, 1862. Notice the similarity between the hull shape of the *Manassas* and the Louisiana State Museum submarine.

(Paul Fleury, et al., *The Soldier in Our Civil War* [New York, 1886].)

The submarine on its side at Spanish Fort with an unidentified man, c. 1895.
Courtesy Wilson and Wanda Gaidry of Residence Plantation.

Louisiana State Museum submarine, Spanish Fort, c. 1895.
Photograph by George F. Mugnier.
(Louisiana State Museum)

Louisiana State Museum submarine on bank of Bayou St. John at Spanish Fort, c. 1900.
(Louisiana State Museum)

At Spanish Fort, 1890s.
Photograph by George F. Mugnier. (Louisiana State Museum)

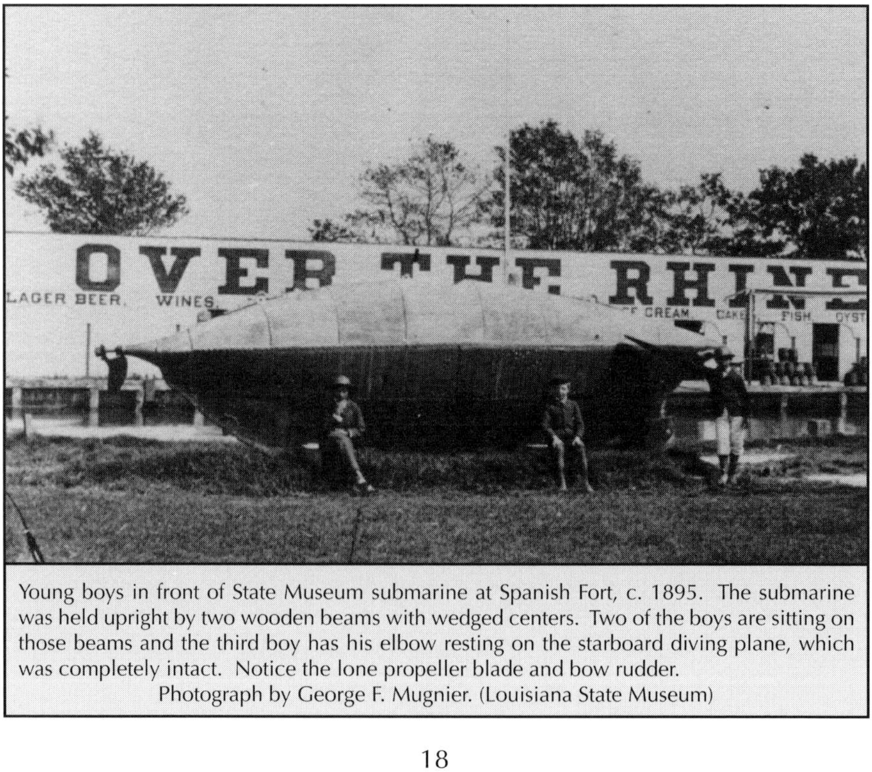

Young boys in front of State Museum submarine at Spanish Fort, c. 1895. The submarine was held upright by two wooden beams with wedged centers. Two of the boys are sitting on those beams and the third boy has his elbow resting on the starboard diving plane, which was completely intact. Notice the lone propeller blade and bow rudder.
Photograph by George F. Mugnier. (Louisiana State Museum)

Easter Festival

. . . and . . .

Presentation of Old Torpedo Boat

At Soldiers' Home

. . . by . . .

Camp Beauregard No. 130, U. S. C. V.

April 10, 1909

Confederate Soldiers Home program for 1909
"Easter Festival and Preservation of Old Torpedo Boat."
Courtesy Dr. Glen Cangelosi.

Ceremony celebrating the move of the submarine from the Confederate Soldiers Home to Jackson Square, 1942.
(Louisiana State Musuem)

After eating their lunch, the children investigate the Confederate submarine in Jackson Square. Climbing on its top are Bruce Casey and Terry Green. Billy Ottendorfer hangs head first as his admiring classmates watch

On display in Jackson Square.
(Louisiana State Musuem)

On display in Jackson Square, c. 1945.
(Louisiana State Musuem)

The submarine being moved into the Pontalba Building Apartment 523 for a "Defense Exhibit," 1953. (Louisiana State Musuem)

This January 1953 photograph shows the submarine in the first floor of the 513 St. Ann Street Pontalba apartment as part of a Louisiana State Museum "Defense Exhibit."
Photograph by Leon Trice, Louisiana State Museum.

State Museum submarine under the Presbytère arcade where it was moved in 1957. This photograph was taken in the mid-1990s. The lighter areas on the lower hull indicate sections that were patched with concrete. Much of the keel had already disintegrated by the time this photograph was taken.

(Louisiana State Musuem)

Louisiana State Museum submarine leaving Presbytère arcade for the conservation lab, December 1999.
(Louisiana State Musuem)

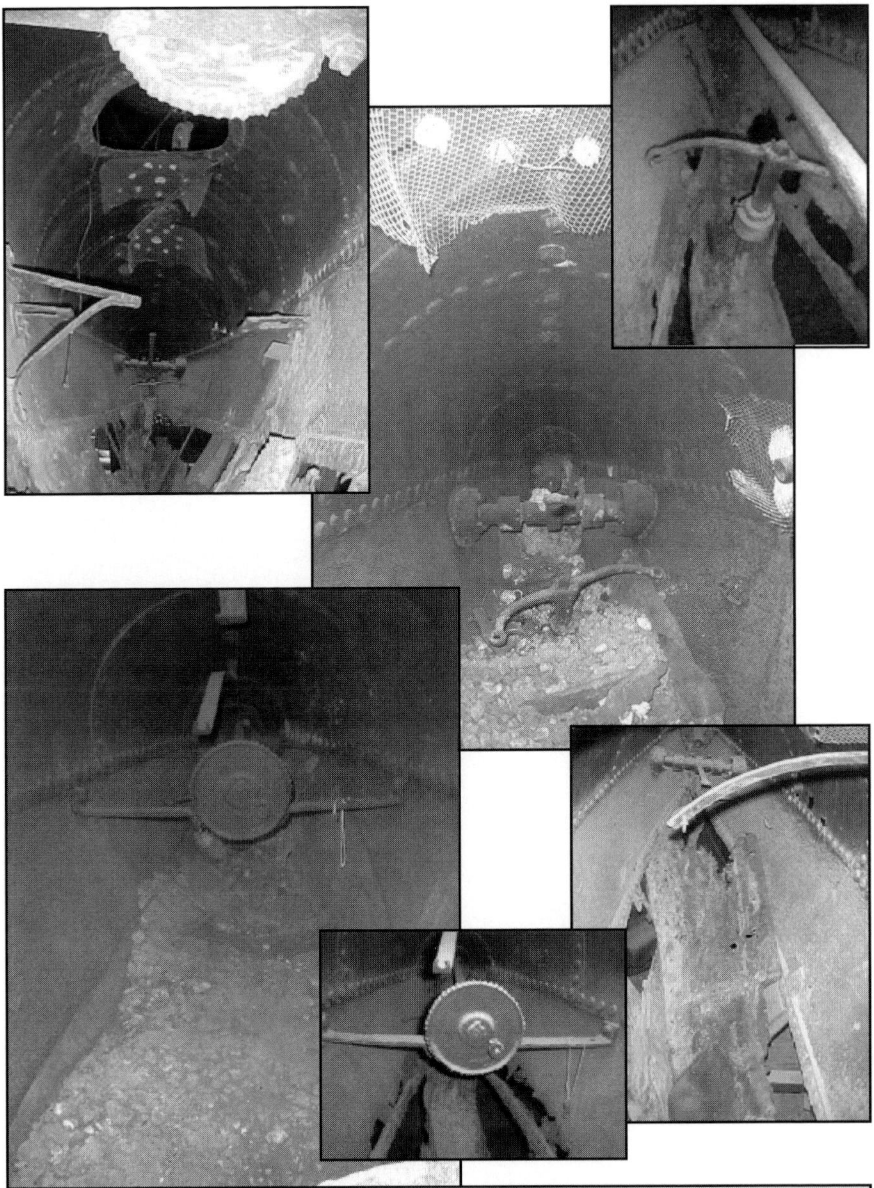

Interior of the submarine before and after concrete was removed from inside the vessel. Note the substantial metal loss that accompanied the concrete's removal. A remaining propeller gear is visible in the immediate foreground. The brackets attached to the sides of the hull were likely used as seats for the crewmen who cranked the propeller shaft. Just forward of the hatchway, a stack opening that was likely used to hold an air hose assembly is also visible. The entire length of the bow rudder shaft can also be seen.
(Louisiana State Musuem)

The Louisiana State Museum submarine in the Baton Rouge museum facility, which opened in early 2006. (Louisiana State Musuem)

For more great history on Louisiana, please visit the properties of the Louisiana State Museum.

IN THE HISTORIC FRENCH QUARTER:

The Cabildo
701 Chartres St., Jackson Square, New Orleans, LA

The Presbytère
751 Chartres St., Jackson Square, New Orleans, LA

The Arsenal
600 St. Peter St., Jackson Square, New Orleans, LA

The 1850 House
523 St. Ann St., Jackson Square, New Orleans, LA

Old U.S. Mint
400 Esplanade Ave., New Orleans, LA

Madame John's Legacy
632 Dumaine St., New Orleans, LA

OUTSIDE OF NEW ORLEANS:

Louisiana State Museum - Patterson
394 Airport Circle Road, Patterson, LA

Old Courthouse Museum
(Louisiana State Museum - Natchitoches)
600 Second Street, Natchitoches, LA

E.D. White Historic Site
2295 La. Hwy. 1, Thibodaux, LA

Louisiana State Museum - Baton Rouge
660 N. Fourth Street, Baton Rouge, LA